BRANCH LINES AROUND WITHAM & KELVEDON

Vic Mitchell

MP Middleton Press

Front cover: Class J69 0-6-0T no. 8636 waits to leave Tollesbury with a train for Kelvedon on 20th June 1948. Light railway station features include a low platform and an old coach body on it. (H.C.Casserley)

Back cover upper: The viaducts on the Maldon branch were all of timber construction. Class J15 no. 65456 is running near Wickham Bishops on 31st May 1958. (Colour-Rail.com.)

Back cover lower: Four-wheeled railbuses prolonged the life of the Maldon branch and one is being loaded at Witham in August 1964. They were also used to Braintree. (B.Pask)

Published August 2010

ISBN 978 1 906008 82 6

© Middleton Press, 2010

Design Deborah Esher

Published by
    Middleton Press
    Easebourne Lane
    Midhurst
    West Sussex
    GU29 9AZ
Tel: 01730 813169
Fax: 01730 812601
Email: info@middletonpress.co.uk
www.middletonpress.co.uk

Printed in the United Kingdom by Henry Ling Limited, at the Dorset Press, Dorchester, DT1 1HD

CONTENTS

INDEX

ACKNOWLEDGEMENTS

I am very grateful for the assistance received from many of those mentioned in the credits also to P.G.Barnes, A.R.Carder, G.Croughton, N.Langridge, B.Lewis, Mr D. and Dr S.Salter, K.Ward and in particular, my very supportive wife, Barbara.

1. Route diagram from the 1947 LNER timetable. The wide lines indicate suburban services.

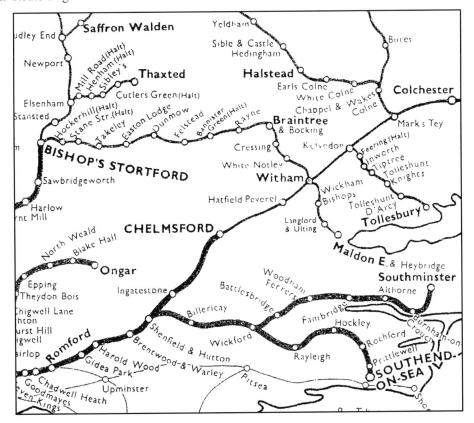

GEOGRAPHICAL SETTING

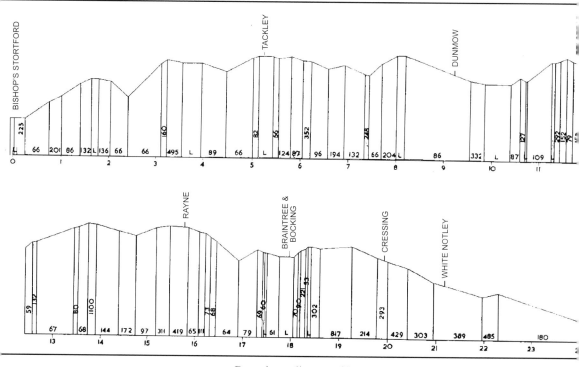

Branch gradient profile.

II. The network is shown on the 1946 survey at 4 miles to 1 inch.

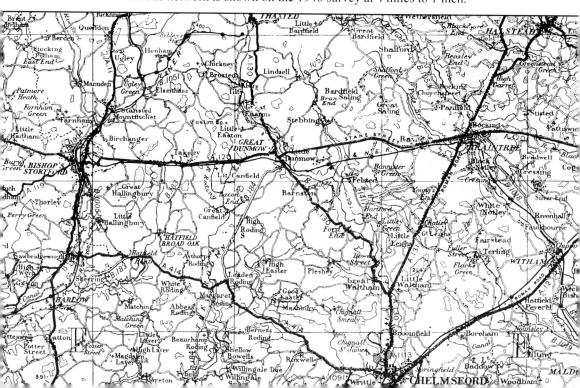

Maldon is at the River Blackwater's first crossing point and was an important commercial centre long before the railways came. It is situated at the confluence of the River Chelmer with the Blackwater. Its small port served a large hinterland in central Essex and was connected to Chelmsford by the Chelmer and Blackwater Navigation.

The routes were entirely in Essex and predominantly on London clay. This was of value for brickmaking. The coastal area is mostly thinly populated, owing to it being marshland. Our east-west route crosses the River Brain at Braintree, the River Chelmer at Dunmow and reaches the River Stort at Bishop's Stortford.

The maps are to the scale of 25ins to 1 mile, with north at the top, unless otherwise indicated.

HISTORICAL BACKGROUND

The Eastern Counties Railway opened between Brentwood and Colchester in 1843. The Northern & Eastern Railway reached Bishop's Stortford from London in 1842 and was extended north to Cambridge in 1845. Later, the two companies became part of the Great Eastern Railway. Both routes had been built to 5ft gauge and were converted to standard in 1844.

The ECR opened a branch from Witham to Maldon on 15th August 1848. Its Act was obtained by the Maldon, Witham & Braintree Railway in 1846. The branch to Braintree came into use on 2nd October 1848.

The Bishop's Stortford, Dunmow & Braintree Act was passed in July 1861 and the route opened on 22nd February 1869. All the lines mentioned came under the control of the GER upon its formation in 1862.

The network of the area was completed when the GER opened a line to Maldon from Woodham Ferrers in 1889, along with its Shenfield-Southend/Southminster branches.

There was a final branch to come, following the Light Railways Act of 1896. The GER obtained an Order for the Kelvedon, Tiptree & Tollesbury Light Railway on 29th January 1901 and traffic commenced on 1st October 1904. A reduced service was provided to Tollesbury Pier from 15th May 1907.

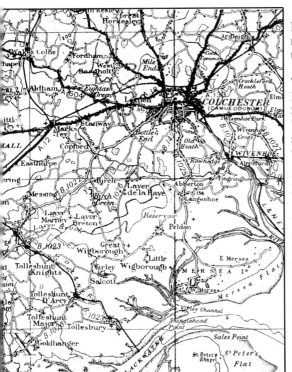

The GER became part of the London & North Eastern Railway in 1923 and this formed most of the Eastern Region of British Railways upon nationalisation in 1948.

Closure to passengers took place thus: Tollesbury-Tollesbury Pier 17th July 1921, Kelvedon-Tollesbury 7th May 1951, Bishop's Stortford-Braintree 3rd March 1952 and Witham-Maldon 7th September 1964. Freight services declined erratically and are detailed in the captions.

Of the routes under review, only the Braintree-Witham section remains open and this was electrified on 3rd October 1977.

Privatisation resulted in the route being branded First Great Eastern on 5th January 1997 when FirstBus was awarded a 7¼ year franchise. This became First Group, but the operation was transferred to National Express, which applied the meaningless name of 'one' from 1st April 2004. It was rebranded National Express East Anglia in 2008.

PASSENGER SERVICES

Bishop's Stortford Branch
The route had a basic service of five trains on most weekdays from the 1880s until World War II. From 1950, the figure increased to 6 or 7. There were also 2 or 3 trains on Sundays at the start of the previous war. Most trains continued to Witham and there was one which ran on to Liverpool Street in 1902, starting at 10.27am.

Braintree Branch
A frequency summary follows, with Sunday trains in brackets. 1848-5(3), 1869-7(2), 1920-8(4), 1950-13(7), 1977-20(0) and 2010-21(17). The latter was effectively hourly.

Only some peak hour trains reached Liverpool Street in the early years of electrification, but from 1981 the majority did so.

Maldon Branch
The summary is 1848-5(3), 1869-5(2), 1925-8(4), 1949-10(5) and 1964-16(12). There were occasional through London trains for weekend visitors, notably in the 1930s and around 1950. Sunday trains were withdrawn in the Winters of the final years.

Tollesbury Branch
The weekday service comprised four weekday trains until 1915, when it increased to five. It had returned to 4 by 1920. Tollesbury Pier was served by two or three trains, if needed. Three trips were normal from the mid-1930s, with only two during part of World War II and after. No Sunday trains were recorded.

1869

December 1902

October 1905

KELVEDON and TOLLESBURY LIGHT.—Great Eastern.
One class only.

Mls		mrn	aft	aft	aft
—	Kelvedon ....dep.	1045	1230	2 45	5 40
—	Inworth........................	Sig.	Sig.	Sig.	Sig.
—	Tiptree........................	11 0	1246	3 1	5 56
—	Tolleshunt D'Arcy	1121	1258	3 13	6 8
—	Tollesbury...................arr.	1126	1 3	3 18	6 13

Mls		mrn	mrn	aft	aft
—	Tollesbury ....dep.	8 25	1140	1 58	6 30
—	Tolleshunt D'Arcy	8 32	1147	2 5	6 41
—	Tiptree........................	8 44	1159	2 17	6 57
—	Inworth........................	Sig.	Sig.	Sig.	Sig.
—	Kelvedon 250. 254 .....arr.	8 59	1214	2 32	7 12

1917 working timetable

KELVEDON AND TOLLESBURY LIGHT RAILWAY.

Single line worked by train staff without tickets, and by only one engine in steam (or two or more engines coupled together).
For regulations for working see Appendix.

Miles from Kelvedon (M. C.)	DOWN WEEK DAYS.		1 Gds.	2 Cars. W R	3 Mxd	4	5 Pass.	6	7 Pass.	8	9 Pass.	10 Pass.	11	12
			a.m.	a.m.	a.m.		a.m.		p.m.		p.m.	p.m.		
— —	Kelvedon	dep.	6 25		9 36		11 30		1 50		5 46	8 5		
— 50	Brooklands Siding...	"	6 30	—	—	—	—	—	—	—	—	—	—	—
2 62	Heath Siding	"	7 0											
2 68	Inworth	"	—	—	*	—	*	—	*	—	*	*	—	—
3 31	Tiptree..............	arr.	7 5		9 45		11 45		2 5		6 1	8 20		
		dep.	7 15	—	9 50	—	11 46	—	2 6	—	6 2	8 21	—	—
3 72	Tudwick Rd. Siding	"	*											
4 5	Tolleshunt Knights	arr.	—	—	*	—	*	—	*	—	*	*	—	—
		dep.												
5 48	Church Siding.........	"	*	—	—	—	—	—	—	—	—	—	—	—
6 45	Tolleshunt D'Arcy	arr.	7 30		10 1		11 57		2 17		6 13	8 32		
		dep.	7 40	—	10 6	—	11 58	—	2 18	—	6 14	8 33	—	—
7 62	Old Hall Siding	"	*											
8 35	Tollesbury	arr.	7 50	—	10 11	—	12 3	—	2 23	—	6 19	8 38	—	—
		dep.		8 5			12 4		2 24		6 20			
9 77	Tollesbury Pier	arr.	—	8 11	—	—	12 10	—	2 30	—	6 26	—	—	—

= 5, 7 & 9 Horse and carriage traffic for Tollesbury only will be conveyed by these trains.
5, 7 & 9 Will run only if required from Tollesbury to Tollesbury Pier, and be passenger or carriage trains as may be necessary. 7 Will run as a mixed train when required.

UP WEEK DAYS.		1 Pass.	2 Mxd	3	4 Pass.	5 Cars.	6 Mxd	7	8 Pass.	9 Gds.	10	11	12
		a.m.	a.m.		p.m.	p.m.	p.m.		p.m.	p.m.			
Tollesbury Pier	dep.	8 5			12 35	2 43			6 19				
Tollesbury	arr.	8 11	—	—	12 41	2 49	—	—	6 25	—	—	—	—
	dep.	8 26	10 32		12 56		3 15		6 39	8 50			
Old Hall Siding	"	—	—	—	—	—	—	—	—	*	—	—	—
Tolleshunt D'Arcy	arr.	8 32	10 38		1 2		3 21		6 45	*			
	dep.	8 33	10 40	—	1 3	—	3 30	—	6 47	—	—	—	—
Church Siding	"									*			
Tolleshunt Knights	arr.	*	*	—	*	—	*	—	*	—	—	—	—
	dep.												
Tudwick Rd. Siding	"	—	—	—	—	—	—	—	—	*	—	—	—
Tiptree..............	arr.	8 44	10 51		1 14		3 46		6 58	*			
	dep.	8 45	10 58	—	1 15	—	4 5	—	7 6	—	—	—	—
Inworth	"	*	*		*		*		*				
Heath Siding	"	—	—	—	—	—	—	—	—	*	—	—	—
Brooklands Siding...	"									*			
Kelvedon	arr.	9 0	11 12	—	1 30	—	4 20	—	7 15	10 6	—	—	—

= 1, 2, 4 & 8 Horse and carriage traffic will be conveyed from Tollesbury only by these trains.
= 1, 4, 5 & 8 Will run only if required from Tollesbury Pier to Tollesbury.

June 1950

BISHOP'S STORTFORD, DUNMOW, and BRAINTREE AND BOCKING

Miles	Week Days only	a.m	a.m	a.m	pm	p.m E	pm S	p.m E	p.m E	p.m S
	4 London (L'poolSt) dep	6A56	8H20	1150	225	4 36	5 0	5 21	6 36	7 20
—	Bishop's Stortford. dep	8 55	9 50	1245	326	5 35	551	6 31	7 35	8 15
1¼	Hockerill Halt..........	8 59	9 54	1249	330	5 39	555	6 35	7 39	8 19
4	Stane Street Halt.......	9 6	10 0	1255	336	5 45	6 1	6 41	7 45	8 25
5½	Takeley................	9 9	10 4	1259	340	5 49	6 5	6 45	7 49	8 29
7¾	Easton Lodge..........	9 14	10 9	1 4	345	5 54	610	6 50	7 54	8 34
9	Dunmow..........[mow	9 20	1015	1 10	350	6 1	615	6 58	8 1	8 41
11¾	Felsted for Little Dun-	9 26	1022	1 16	356	6 7	621	7 4	8 7	8 47
13¾	Bannister Green Halt...	9 31	1027	1 20	4 1	6 12	626	7 9	8 12	8 52
15¾	Rayne..................	9 37	1033	1 26	4 7	6 18	632	7 15	8 18	8 58
18	Braintree & Bocking arr	9 42	1038	1 31	412	6 23	637	7 20	8 24	9 4

Week Days only	a.m	am	a.m	p.m	pm E	p.m E	p.m S	p.m
Braintree & Bocking dep	6 46	739	10 50	2 0	326	4 30	4 50	6d35
Rayne..................	6 54	745	10 56	2 6	332	4 36	4 56	6d41
Bannister Green Halt...	6 58	749	11 0	2 10	336	4 40	5 0	6d45
Felsted for Little Dun-	7 4	754	11 6	2 15	342	4 46	5 6	6d50
Dunmow ....[mow	7 11	8 2	11 14	2 22	351	4 54	5 14	6d57
Easton Lodge..........	7 17	8 8	11 20	2 28	357	5 0	5 20	7d 3
Takeley................	7 22	813	11 25	2 33	4 2	5 5	5 25	7d 8
Stane Street Halt	7 25	816	11 28	2 36	4 5	5 8	5 28	7d11
Hockerill Halt..........	7 31	822	11 34	2 42	411	5 14	5 34	7E17
Bishop's Stortford. arr	7 34	825	11 37	2 45	414	5 17	5 37	7 20
4 London(L'poolSt) arr	8 50	924	12P36	5B 0	6 0	6J45	6 45	8 45

A Passengers can dep. 7 6 a.m. Third class only
B Arr. 5 3 p.m. on Saturdays
E or E Except Saturdays
d 3 minutes later on Saturdays
H Dep. 8 24 a.m. on Fridays and Saturdays
J Arr. 6 55 p.m. on Fridays
P Arr. 12 43 p.m. on Saturdays
S Saturdays only

Tickets from the Halts and Easton Lodge issued on train
Passengers to or from Stane Street and Bannister Green Halts must travel in special car provided

September 1950

KELVEDON and TOLLESBURY (Light Railway)—(One class only)

Miles	Week Days only	a.m		p.m			
—	Kelvedon ....dep	1010	..	5 45	..	..	..
¾	Feering Halt........	1013	..	5 48	..	..	..
2¾	Inworth............	1020	..	5 55	..	..	..
3¾	Tiptree............	1029	..	6 4	..	..	..
4	Tolleshunt Knights.	1033	..	6 8	..	..	..
6¼	Tolleshunt D'Arcy..	1045	..	6 20	..	..	..
8¼	Tollesbury ..... arr	1050	..	6 25	..	..	..

Miles	Week Days only	a.m		p.m		p.m
—	Tollesbury ..... dep	8 30	..	1250	..	6 37
2	Tolleshunt D'Arcy..	8 38	..	1 5	..	6 50
4½	Tolleshunt Knights.	8 44	..	1 11	..	6 56
5	Tiptree............	8 54	..	1 35	..	7 7
5¾	Inworth	8 57	..	1 38	..	7 10
8	Feering Halt	9 5	..	1 46	..	7 18
8¼	Kelvedon .... arr	9 9	..	1 50	..	7 22

Tickets (single only) and Local Tickets are issued on the train

1. Bishop's Stortford Branch
BISHOP'S STORTFORD

III.   The 1939 edition has a granary to the southwest of the goods sheds. Nearby, Cr. marks the location of the crane, which was rated at 7-ton capacity. North of Station Road bridge is a short siding, which served a granary. North of this is North Box which controlled the junction for the Braintree branch. The circles nearby are the gas holders of the Bishop's Stortford, Epping & District Gas Company. Its private siding and weighing machines are shown, along with its wharf.

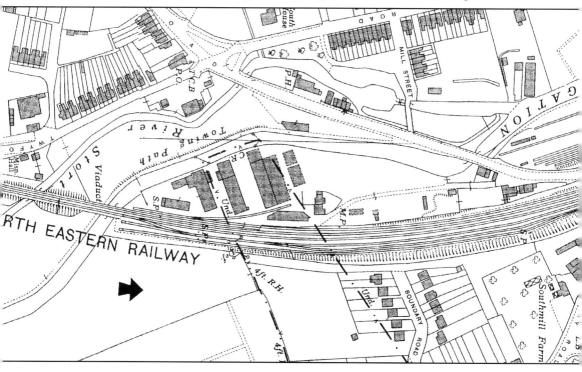

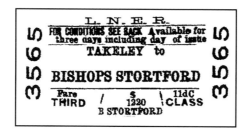

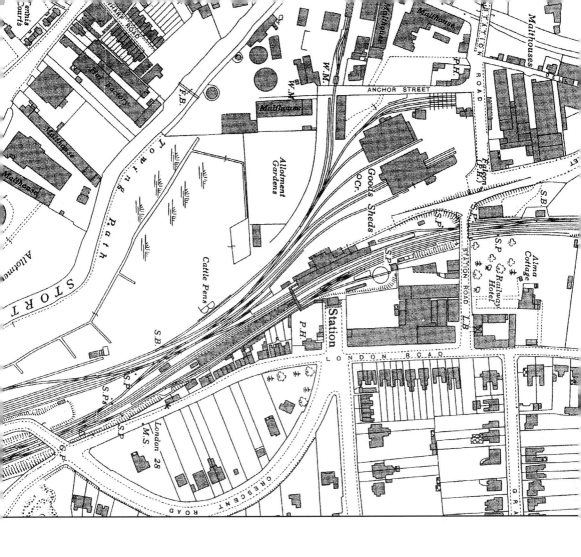

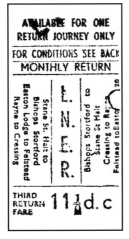

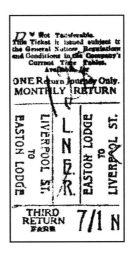

1.   A postcard view north has the down platform in the distance, the footbridge being at the extremity of the platforms. The main building is beyond it. (P.Laming coll.)

2.   We look north again, but this time from the road bridge near the join in the map. The structure carries London Road. South Box is centre in this view from 23rd February 1952 and on the left is class N7 0-6-2T no. 69713. North Box closed on 13th August 1960 and South Box took over its work. (J.H.Meredith)

3.   Seen on the same day is a train from London, hauled by class L1 2-6-4T no. 67729. To the left of the train is the up main line and parallel to that is the Braintree branch. It ran close to the main lines, but at an increasingly higher level, for about ¾ mile, before curving sharply east. (D.T.Rowe)

4.   A similar panorama from 20th April 1958 shows all of the down platform and a class N7 standing on the short siding, which was only 180ft in length. On the left is "Britannia" class 4-6-2 no. 70003 *John Bunyan*. To the left of that, another engine stands on the turntable. The locomotive allocation was seven in 1939. Coded 30C in 1949-59, the site closed in November 1960. (RAS Marketing)

5.   Just prior to electrification of the Liverpool Street route in 1960, the up platforms were extended north, as shown. Also evident is the new footbridge, which included luggage lifts for parcels traffic. (N.R.Sprinks)

6.   The down side facilities are seen in February 1969, with the new ticket hall contrasting with the earlier structures. (F.Hornby)

NORTH OF BISHOP'S STORTFORD

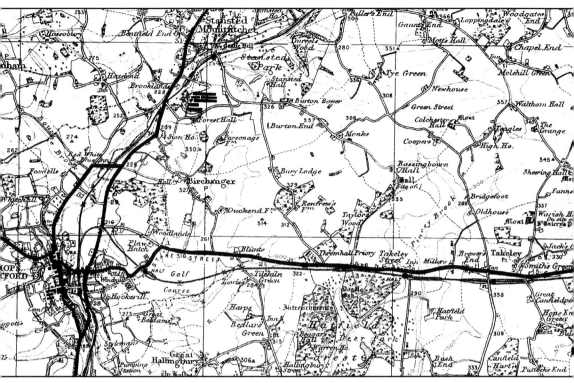

IV.   The 1930 revision has the Braintree branch on the right and the A11 running north-south, east of the centre of the town. Road numbering was introduced in 1919, after so many Army vehicles had difficulties. The scale is 1ins to 1 mile.

7.   A Brush Type 2 diesel is southbound in 1959, as class J20/1 0-6-0 no. 64691 nears the end of its journey on the branch with a freight train. Electrification from London took place on 16th November 1960 and extension to Cambridge followed on 10th June 1986. The posts are ready in good time.
(A.J.Pike/F.Hornby coll.)

HOCKERILL HALT

8.   The platform came into use on 7th November 1910 for the benefit of the members of the nearby golf club, which had its course both sides of the railway. The public were soon allowed to use the halt and steps were provided from the road; the photographer is at the top of them. There was a siding for the Government Cold Storage Depot ¼ mile west of the halt, on the north side, from 1942 until 1967. The London Railway Society stored stock there prior to its transfer to Quainton Road. (P.Laming coll.)

9.   This is another view east and passengers were initially only allowed to travel to and from this direction, but had to buy Bishop's Stortford tickets. This did not apply after 1922, as guards could collect fares thereafter. (D.T.Rowe)

STANE STREET HALT

10.   The halt was on the south side of the line and was opened on 18th December 1922. The guard extended retractable steps near his compartment and he also lit the oil lamp when necessary. Both halts are shown on the last map. (D.T.Rowe)

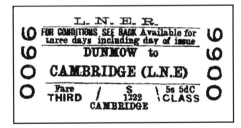

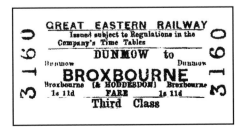

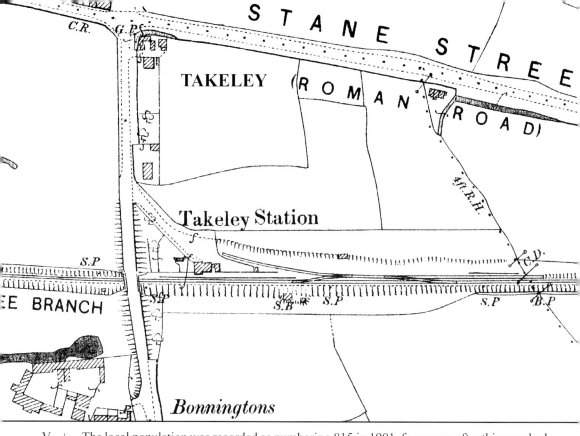

C.R. G.P.S

STANE STREET

TAKELEY (ROMAN ROAD)

4f R.H.

Takeley Station

S.P

EE BRANCH

S.P

S.B

S.P

G.D

S.P

B.P

Bonningtons

V. ' The local population was recorded as numbering 815 in 1901, four years after this map had been published. The bridge carried the road to Hatfield Broad Oak. At the time of closure, there were 1196 residents.

11. Class F5 no. 67211 stands with a train destined for Witham. The loop in the foreground does not show on the maps, as it was added in 1927. (D.T.Rowe)

12.   The signal box (right) had 24 levers and was closed on 9th August 1966. In the distance is the cattle dock. The goods yard remained in use until 11th April 1966. (Lens of Sutton coll.)

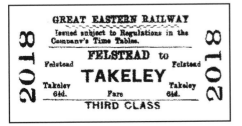

GREAT EASTERN RAILWAY
Issued subject to Regulations in the
Company's Time Tables.
FELSTEAD to
Felstead   Felstead
TAKELEY
Takeley   Takeley
6½d.   Fare   6½d.
THIRD CLASS
2018   2018

GREAT EASTERN RAILWAY.
ONE BICYCLE (Accompanied by Passenger)
At Company's limited risk rate.
DUNMOW   to
ANY STATION ON THE G. E. Ry.
NOT EXCEEDING 50 MILES
ZONE 50.   Rate 1s. 0d.
Available for a single journey and on the day of issue
only & must be given up on completion of journey.
[For conditions see back]
0033   0033

EASTON LODGE

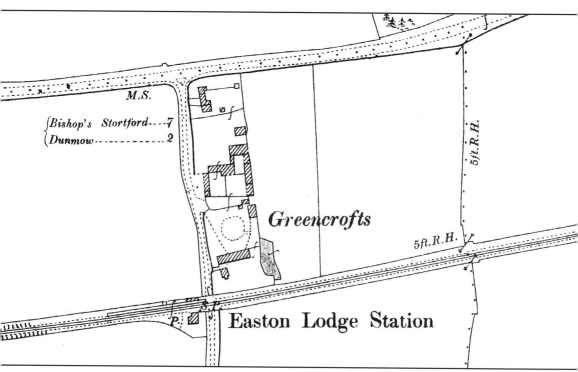

VI. The station opened a little later than the others, on 2nd September 1895 and is seen on the 1897 edition.

13. The Earl and Countess of Warwick lived nearby and the latter partially funded the station. Staffing ceased in about 1928. The signals were to protect the level crossing. A loop was laid down beyond this in 1942 and four sidings ran from it to a US airfield. Two of these served Geest Bananas from 1962 until all traffic ceased on the branch on 17th February 1972.
(P.Laming coll.)

14.   The low lamp was to light the steps up to the platform. The term "Halt" was used sometimes, but there is no evidence of it in this late photograph. (D.T.Rowe)

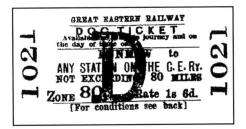

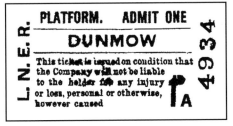

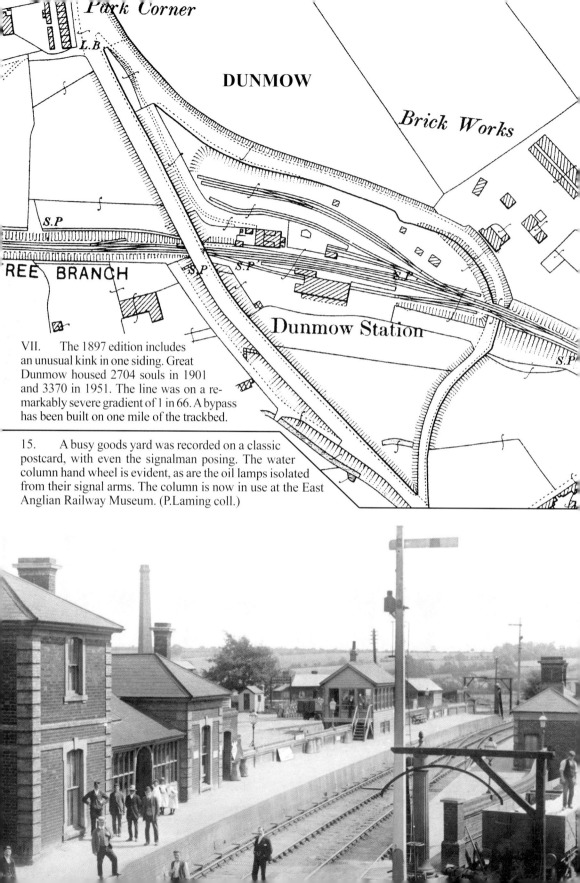

DUNMOW

Park Corner

L.B

Brick Works

S.P

REE BRANCH

S.P

S.P

S.P

Dunmow Station

S.P

VII.	The 1897 edition includes
an unusual kink in one siding. Great
Dunmow housed 2704 souls in 1901
and 3370 in 1951. The line was on a re-
markably severe gradient of 1 in 66. A bypass
has been built on one mile of the trackbed.

15.	A busy goods yard was recorded on a classic
postcard, with even the signalman posing. The water
column hand wheel is evident, as are the oil lamps isolated
from their signal arms. The column is now in use at the East
Anglian Railway Museum. (P.Laming coll.)

16.   A panorama from 9th September 1962 reveals that many details have changed; even the chimney of the brickworks has gone. Behind the camera was a siding to the Dunmow Flitch Bacon Factory and on the north side of the line was one to a corn and seed mill. In 1938, 678 tons of bacon were despatched, plus around 1400 tons of flour and grain. (R.M.Casserley)

17.   Just out of view on the left was a 30cwt crane. Although regular passenger trains ceased in 1952, an occasional excursion ran until August 1964. Goods traffic ceased on 19th September 1967. The box had 35 levers, nine of which were spare, and it closed on the same day, having been a ground frame latterly. The station was demolished and the trackbed was used for the Dunmow bypass. (Lens of Sutton coll.)

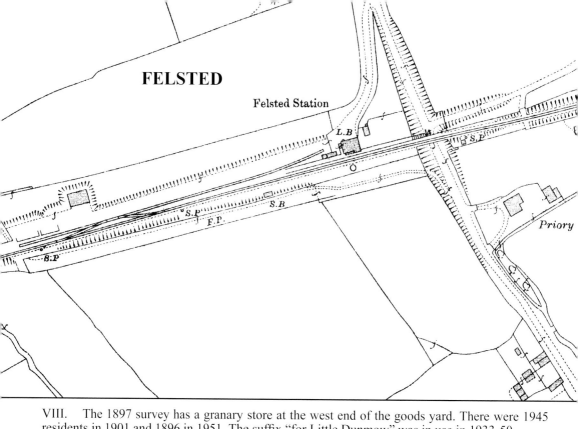

FELSTED

Felsted Station

L.B

S.P

S.B

S.P

F.P

S.P

Priory

VIII.   The 1897 survey has a granary store at the west end of the goods yard. There were 1945 residents in 1901 and 1896 in 1951. The suffix "for Little Dunmow" was in use in 1933-50.

18.   The nameboard shows the A used by the railways until 5th June 1950. A goods loop was added in the foreground in 1926-27. Note the simple telegraph system in this view from about 20 years earlier. (P.Laming coll.)

19.   We can now enjoy four photographs from 23rd February 1952. Class F5 2-4-2T no. 67196 is bound for Bishop's Stortford with the usual two coaches. When the loop was completed, a siding was laid from it in 1926 to a sugar beet factory, behind the camera. (J.H.Meredith)

20.   No. 67198 is of the same class and is heading the 9.50am Bishop's Stortford to Braintree service. The signal box had a 24-lever frame. The line west of Felsted to Dunmow was the first section of the route to be closed completely. This took place on 10th April 1966, due to the poor condition of the Chelmer Viaduct at Langleys, just to the east of Dunmow station. It was demolished in 1977. (J.H.Meredith)

21.   The British Sugar Corporation's private siding gate was near the left border of the map. Andrew Barclay built this 0-4-0ST for the new works and it operated there until the route to Braintree closed on 20th June 1970. Latterly, it was a standby engine for a Ruston & Hornsby diesel. (J.H.Meredith)

22.   The beet transfer work was undertaken by a Taylor & Hibbard crane for many years. There were four parallel double ended sidings connected to three more similar ones. The factory closed in 1981. (J.H.Meredith)

23.   Class J16 0-6-0 no. 65536 was photographed running eastwards. The goods yard here closed on 6th May 1964. Redundant rolling stock from the factory was moved to the BSC Works at Foley Park, near Kidderminster. (D.T.Rowe)

BANNISTER GREEN HALT

24. This was the second halt on the route to be opened on 18th December 1922 in an attempt to deal with bus competition. The bridge carried the B1417 Felsted to Rayne road.
(D.T.Rowe)

25. The low platform was on the south side of the line and it required agile passengers. There are steps on the train for them and others for the lamp lighter. They are seen on 1st March 1952.
(D.T.Rowe)

RAYNE

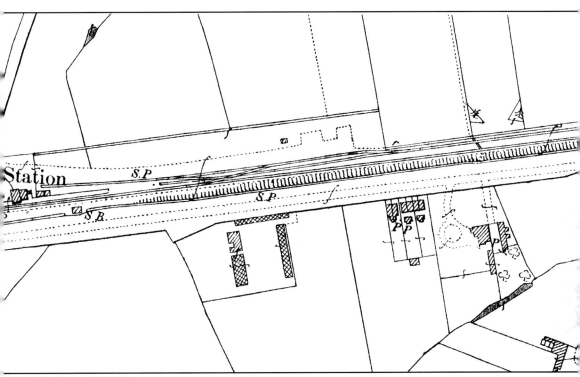

IX.   The 1897 edition includes glasshouses south of the line, but few houses. There were 387 souls in the village in 1901, the figure rising to 761 in 1961.

26.   The signal box had 12 levers and is seen with class J16 0-6-0 no. 65536 in 1952. The route here is on a gradient of 1 in 419. (D.T.Rowe)

27.   The box ceased to be a block post in 1927, but could set a freight train aside in the goods yard. The main buildings were similar to others on the route and are seen on 4th September 1962. (H.C.Casserley)

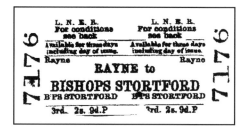

28.   The view west was recorded on the same day. Although it is ten years since the last passenger left, the lamp and nameboard are in good order. There was a staff of seven in 1906. (R.M.Casserley)

29.   After years of dereliction, the fine building was restored in 1994 for use as an information centre. It is seen in January 1991; part of the trackbed became the Flitch Way for recreation. (Dr I.C.Scotchman)

2. Braintree Branch
BRAINTREE

X. The 1897 map unexpectedly includes two silk mills and a Lower Railway Street. The crane (C.) was rated at 5-tons. Crittall Windows later became an important railway customer, their factory being built immediately west of the malthouse. The east end of the brickworks site developed as a coal depot and an extra siding was laid. The goods station had been the terminus of the branch from Witham from 1848 until 1869. Crittalls and the gasworks had private sidings from 1918.

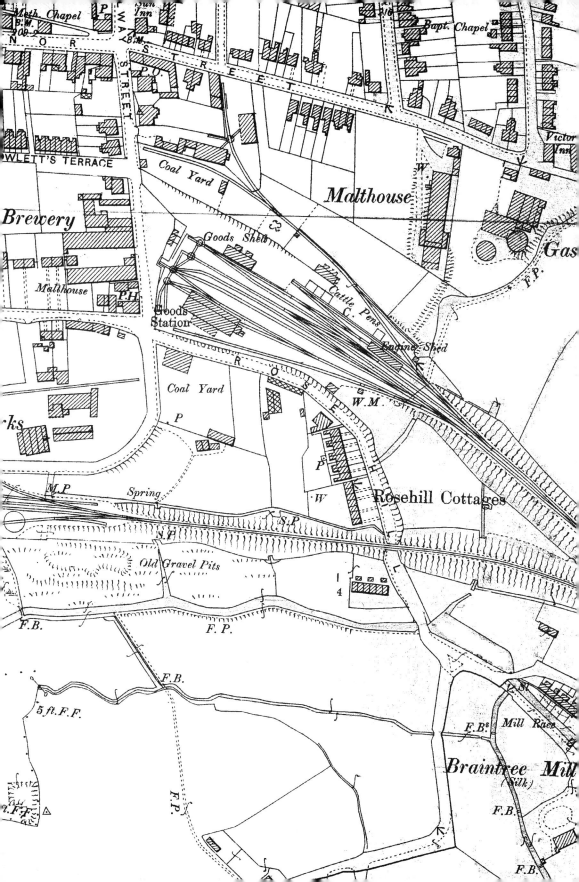

30.   We approach the station from the west in about 1900 and can examine one of the GER's rotary ground signals. The line behind us continues to Rayne, while the one on the left is part of a long siding. (Lens of Sutton coll.)

31.   Moving closer to the station, we see a train from Witham near the end of the single line from Braintree Goods Junction. The GER had designated this section as "down", but the LNER changed it to "up". Local produce is much in evidence. (Lens of Sutton coll.)

32.   The north elevation presented a good impression to the town, which grew from 8670 residents in 1901 to 20,970 in 1961. These figures include Bocking. (P.Laming coll.)

33.   Class F4 2-4-2T no. 7574 accelerates the 6.28pm departure for Bishop's Stortford on 20th July 1938. The coaches are six-wheelers. There were 11 private sidings listed that year. (D.T.Rowe)

34.   The branch train from Witham has just terminated on 16th February 1952, with steam from the heating system evident. The locomotive is class F5 2-4-2T no. 67198. (F.Hornby)

35.   The term "& Bocking" was in use from 19th October 1910 to 6th May 1968, but it was not applied to the end of the signal box. This had 30 levers and closed on 12th June 1977. It was soon moved to Chappel & Wakes Colne for use by the Stour Valley Railway Preservation Society. (A.Vaughan coll.)

36.   The 45ft turntable was photographed on 8th September 1955. It was seldom used by locomotives by that time, but the area was convenient for a permanent way site. (J.H.Meredith)

37.   Class F5 no. 67189 has just arrived from Witham on 22nd September 1956. The platform on the right had not been required for four years and the footbridge to it has been partially dismantled. (B.Pask)

38. Railbuses were used in 1958-63; these are illustrated later. Here is one of the subsequent DMUs, used until electrification. One presumes that there was a passenger with a mobility problem. (Lens of Sutton coll.)

39. Electrification in 1977 brought class 312 units and a single track. The photograph is from 30th August 1982, when facilities were still provided for gentlemen, despite other cutbacks. (T.Heavyside)

BRAINTREE GOODS

40.   Braintree Goods Junction signal box closed in 1927 and this ground frame sufficed thereafter.
A train staff could be released from the box adjacent. The foundry of Lake & Elliot Ltd (right) dated
from 1917 and its private siding received coal and scrap metal. These three photographs are from
12th January 1991. (Dr I.C.Scotchman)

41.   The engine shed (see map) had five locomotives in 1922 and three in 1939 and closed in November 1959. In 1977, there was a goods train each weekday from Temple Mills and one on Sundays from Ince to the Shellstar Fertiliser Depot, which is on the right. The old goods shed is on the left. Some freight traffic ceased on 10th April 1975, when the foundry siding closed. (Dr I.C.Scotchman)

42.   The original terminal building was for long used as the goods office and finally as a coal office. The public goods service was withdrawn on 1st August 1978, leaving only fertiliser traffic. (Dr. I.C.Scotchman)

BRAINTREE FREEPORT

43.   The station opened on 8th November 1999 and served a new shopping complex. No. 321441 is working the 14.06 Braintree to Witham on 16th January 2000. (Dr I.C.Scotchman)

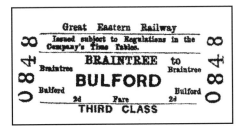

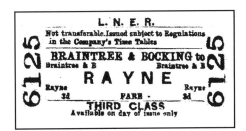

CRESSING

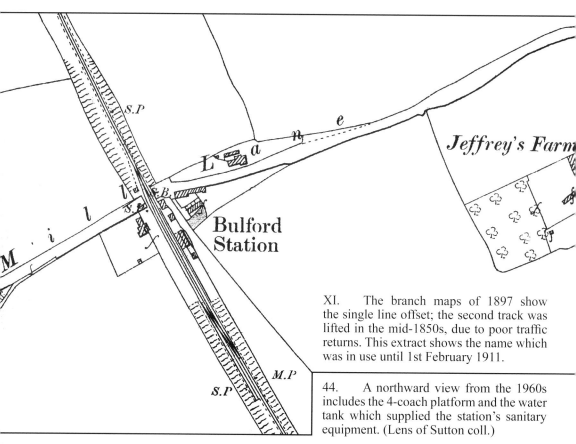

Mill Lane

S.P

Bulford
Station

Jeffrey's Farm

M.P

S.P

XI.   The branch maps of 1897 show
the single line offset; the second track was
lifted in the mid-1850s, due to poor traffic
returns. This extract shows the name which
was in use until 1st February 1911.

44.   A northward view from the 1960s
includes the 4-coach platform and the water
tank which supplied the station's sanitary
equipment. (Lens of Sutton coll.)

CRESSING

45.   The goods yard remained open until 7th September 1964 and the signal box was in use until electrification of services. It was removed to Castle Hedingham by the Colne Valley Railway Preservation Society soon after. (Lens of Sutton coll.)

46.   No. 321351 arrives on 31st May 2010 while working the 15.00 Braintree to Liverpool Street. The platform length was increased to take eight cars, early in 1993. Tickets were issued here until about 1995 and the gates were replaced by barriers on 18th May 1997. (Dr I .C.Scotchman)

WHITE NOTLEY

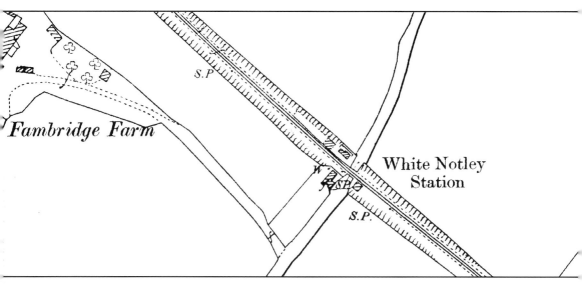

XII.   The village was recorded as having 335 residents in 1901 and 500 in 1961. The station opened in October 1853.

47.   The approach to the station was rural indeed and is seen in the presence of a car of 1920s vintage. (P.Laming coll.)

48.   This early postcard has the station building on the right and the house for the station master prominent. The white diamond indicates the health of the signalling to the driver. (P.Laming coll.)

49.   The glass bowl of an oil lamp is evident in this 1960s record. Don't miss the portable steps for those with limited mobility; no handrail though, unlike those on the GWR. (Lens of Sutton coll.)

50.	There was rural charm with a summer house style waiting room. The wicket gate was for use by impatient pedestrians. The main gates were operated by hand by a man who also issued tickets until about 1995. (Lens of Sutton coll.)

51.	The station was rebuilt in 1977 and provision made for 4 cars, this being subsequently increased to 8 and then 12 cars. The 13.48 Liverpool Street to Braintree was worked by no. 321351 on 31st May 2010. Lifting barriers came into use on 26th May 1997. (Dr I.C.Scotchman)

WITHAM

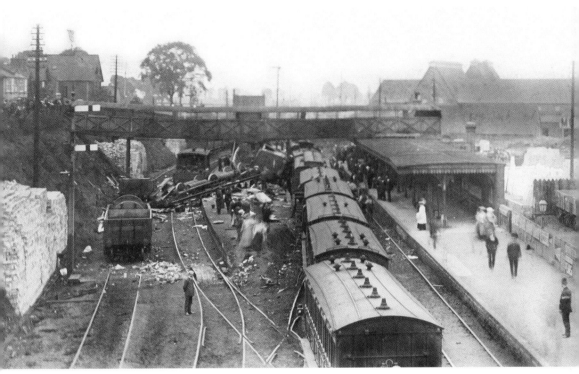

52.   The oldest picture on offer is the saddest. A down Cromer express came to grief on 1st September 1905 alongside the island platform, as rebuilding was in progress. The rear 11 of a 14-coach train derailed at 70mph. Eight passengers and a porter died due to a track defect. (P.Laming coll.)

53.   A later postcard view of the same location shows a new footbridge over the two main lines and a new ticket office over the down loop (left). The platforms are numbered 1 to 4 from south to north. Empty milk churns abound. (P.Laming coll.)

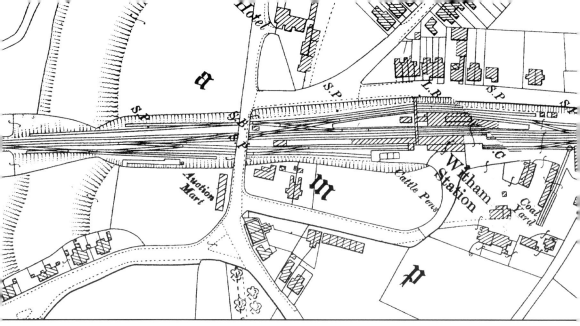

XIII.   The 1897 survey has the Braintree branch at the top (with the track offset on the first bridge) and the Maldon one at the bottom. The right part of the triangle was out of use by that time and is disconnected at its north end, which was termed Witham East. The turntable was 42ft long and is at the top.

54.   A 2-4-2T Class F5 is entering Witham from Braintree on 25th September 1956 and in the background is Baird's Malting. The Witham plant is currently the largest of the Baird's malting sites with a total annual production of around 46,000 tonnes. The premises were established in 1926 when a 'traditional' floor maltings was built. (B.Pask)

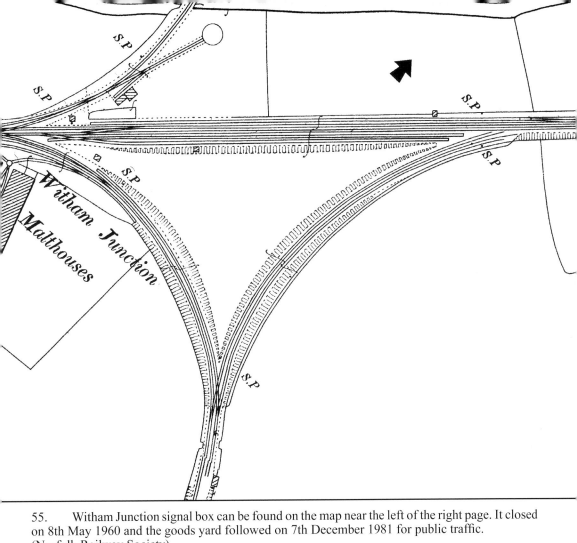

55.   Witham Junction signal box can be found on the map near the left of the right page. It closed on 8th May 1960 and the goods yard followed on 7th December 1981 for public traffic. (Norfolk Railway Society)

56.   Class F5 2-4-2T no. 67196 has just run in front of the signal box as it approaches platform 4. A down main line train is signalled. (D.T.Rowe)

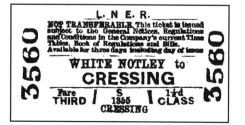

57.　　Another down main line train is signalled as a railbus rounds the curve on the Maldon line. The 10 sign refers to the speed limit on the curve at the start of the Braintree branch and the T to the termination of a temporary speed restriction on the down main line. (Norfolk Railway Society)

58.　　The Maldon railbus stands on the loop beyond the platform 1 line. Similar vehicles were built in Britain by AC Cars; those used in Essex were of German origin. (Norfolk Railway Society)

59.   The destination is obvious as a DMU waits at platform 4. Its driving compartment is under the ticket office. (Norfolk Railway Society)

60.   We move forward to 30th August 1982 and find no. 312795 at platform 4 (left) bound for Braintree, while no. 312782 calls with a Liverpool Street to Clacton-on-Sea service. (T.Heavyside)

61.   Under the ticket office on 22nd March 2003 is no. 321312 forming the 12.32 Liverpool Street to Braintree. There was an hourly such service by that time. (T.Heavyside)

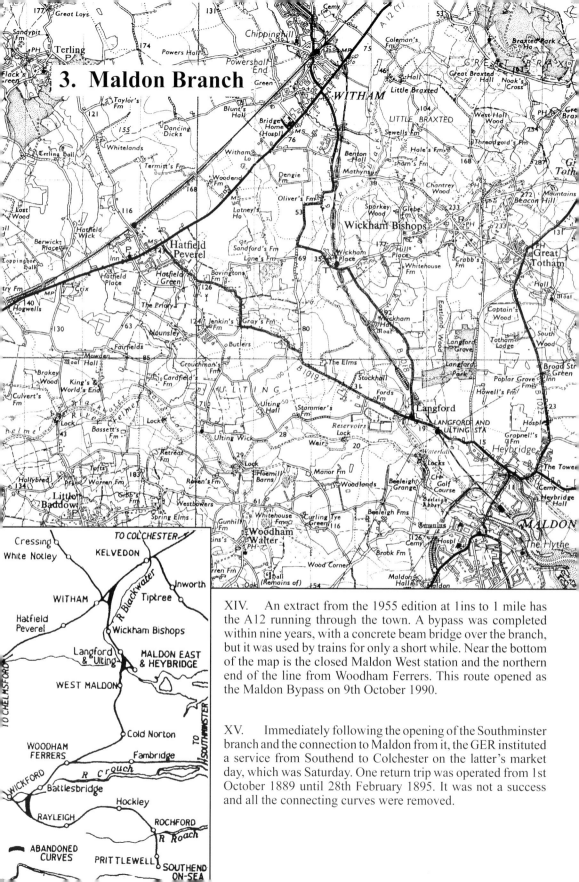

3. Maldon Branch

XIV. An extract from the 1955 edition at 1ins to 1 mile has the A12 running through the town. A bypass was completed within nine years, with a concrete beam bridge over the branch, but it was used by trains for only a short while. Near the bottom of the map is the closed Maldon West station and the northern end of the line from Woodham Ferrers. This route opened as the Maldon Bypass on 9th October 1990.

XV. Immediately following the opening of the Southminster branch and the connection to Maldon from it, the GER instituted a service from Southend to Colchester on the latter's market day, which was Saturday. One return trip was operated from 1st October 1889 until 28th February 1895. It was not a success and all the connecting curves were removed.

EAST OF WITHAM

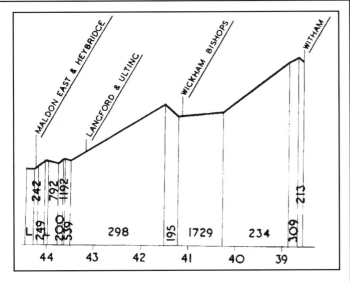

62.   The A12 once passed through the centre of the town and the Maldon branch ran under it at Colchester Road bridge. South of it was Rom River Steel Stockyard and its Hibberd "Planet" was photographed on 13th April 1977, with the vestige of the Maldon branch in the background.
(Dr I.C.Scotchman)

Gradient Profile.

WICKHAM BISHOPS

XVI. The word "Bishops" was added to the station name to distinguish it from Wickham near Fareham, in Hampshire.

63. The station was unusual in having the path to the platform across a goods siding. Another case was at Combpyne and is shown in *Branch Line to Lyme Regis*. (P.Laming coll.)

64.   The neglected signal box had last been used in 1932 and is seen on 10th August 1957. Like the Braintree branch, the track was laid double, but soon singled. It remained offset. (B.Pask)

65.   The signal box still carried its name when photographed around 1960. The mill is in the background and note that the station is at ground level, not that of the platform. (Lens of Sutton coll.)

66.   Railbuses ran on both branches from Witham from July 1958. While they were fuel efficient, they presented problems with parcels traffic and perambulators. The house remains in use as a dwelling today. (Lens of Sutton coll.)

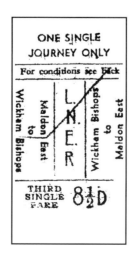

67.   The railbuses built by Waggon und Maschinenbau in Germany, weighed 15 tons and seated 56. Examples survive on the North Norfolk Railway and the Keighley & Worth Valley Railway. There were several timber trestle bridges in use on the branch and one has recently been restored. (Lens of Sutton coll.)

68.   The goods yard here closed the same day as branch passenger service ceased, 7th September 1964. This is the view soon after. (Lens of Sutton coll.)

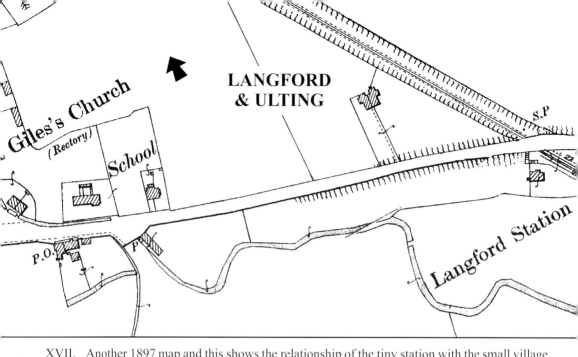

XVII.   Another 1897 map and this shows the relationship of the tiny station with the small village. The suffix was added on 1st July 1923 to avoid confusion with a Somerset station shown in *Branch Lines around Cheddar*.

69.   Few station buildings could claim a full length bench seat and also no railway information on display. The map shows a signal box, but there is no evidence of it in available photographs. It closed in December 1919. (Lens of Sutton coll.)

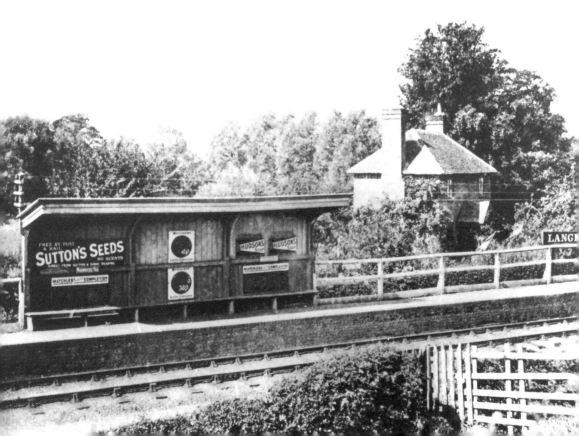

70.   Arriving with a train from Witham on 11th August 1957 is class F5 no. 67195. Nationalisation has brought some timetables for display. The bridge carries the B1090. (B.Pask)

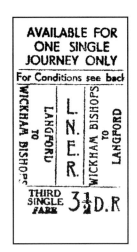

MALDON EAST & HEYBRIDGE

XVIII. The 1874 survey has the canal wharf siding top left. It is on the Chelmer & Blackwater Navigation. The siding to the river wharf is lower centre. The two road crossings are explained in caption 80.

Turn Table

Gasometer

B.M. 21·9?

FULLBRIDGE

Fullbridge House

Timber Yard

Coal Yard

UPPER DOCK

Wharf

ill Bridge

Wharf

Wharf

STATION

Station

Coal Yard

Rayleigh Wharf

Railway

Coal Yard

Dock Wharf

ROAD

LOWER DOCK

71.   A view from the engine shed line on 18th October 1952 features class F5 2-4-2T no. 67191. The station gained the suffix "East" in 1889, when the line from the south opened, and "& Heybridge" on 1st October 1907. (D.T.Rowe)

Other views of this station can be found in
Branch Lines to Southend and Southminster, **pictures 81 to 84.**

72.   The impressive terminus was photographed in 1954. After the last passenger left ten years later, it would be another ten years of neglect before restoration began. It became a public house and restaurant; it was used for commercial purposes from 1999. (B.Connel/H.Davies)

73.   This is the view towards Witham, with the stub of the wharf siding on the right and the girders of the bridge over the Chelmer & Blackwater Navigation in the centre. Curving left in the distance is the line south, which was used for wagon storage in its later years. Passenger service on it ceased in 1939. (Norfolk Railway Society)

74.   Goods traffic lasted until 18th April 1966 and the site became an industrial estate. The large goods shed (left) was incorporated into it. The water column is at the end of the platform. (Norfolk Railway Society)

75.   The short platform (right) had a run-round loop, from which there is a line to a loading dock. All nameboards were removed during World War II and it seems that this one was lost, as a tiny replacement is in place. The date is 26th May 1956. (H.C.Casserley)

76.   Seen in 1958, the engine shed had its water tank under the pitched roof. The town's supply was found to have double the safe level of fluoride and so residents had brown teeth, but no decay. Dilution from other sources followed and there are no records of boiler problems. The shed closed on 2nd November 1959. (B.Pask)

77.   The signal box was built in 1889, between the canal and road crossings. Class J15 0-6-0 no. 65447 arrives in July 1958 and passes the south end of the former canal wharf siding. The 62-lever box was in use until branch closure on 18th April 1966 and was destroyed at the end of 1979. (B.Pask)

78.   The south end of the yard was photographed in July 1958, along with the ground frame box. There had earlier been a turntable to the left of it. (B.Pask)

79.   The goods shed is in the distance in this northward view, not long before closure. The seat has been repositioned to deflect the myopic from the group of retired barrows. (Dr G.B.Sutton)

80.   Conventional DMUs appeared in the last year of operation. This one has just run over the level crossing, adjacent to which was an underpass, with only 9ft headroom. The cameraman is standing on its ironwork. (A.Ingram)

4. Kelvedon Branch
KELVEDON LOW LEVEL

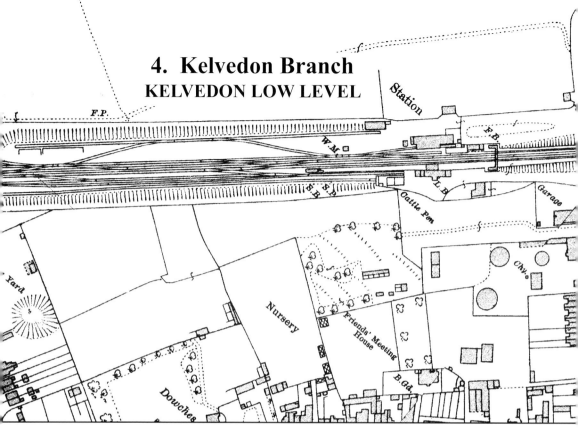

XIX.   The 1923 extract is just north of the town centre and has the main line station on the left page and the branch one on the right. Near the page boundary is Station Road and the River Blackwater, which runs roughly parallel to the main line from Witham.

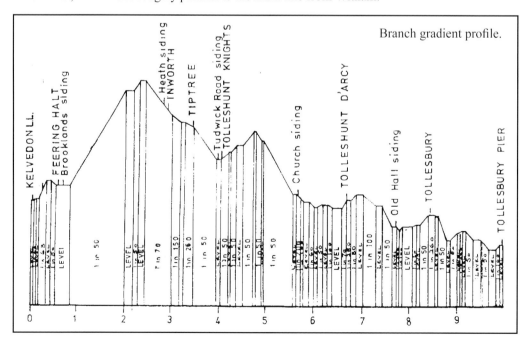

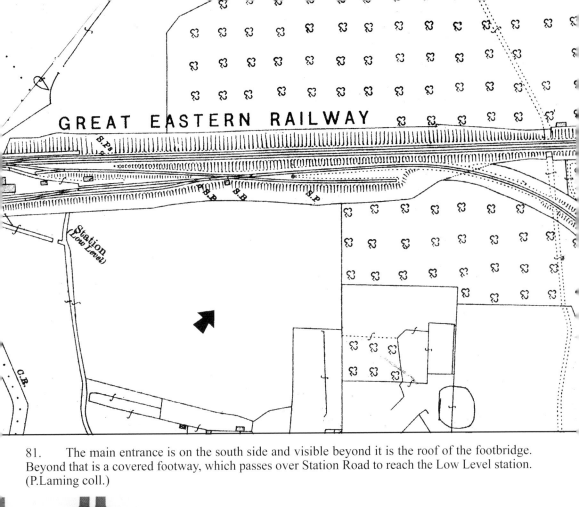

GREAT EASTERN RAILWAY

Station
(Low Level)

G.B.

81.   The main entrance is on the south side and visible beyond it is the roof of the footbridge. Beyond that is a covered footway, which passes over Station Road to reach the Low Level station. (P.Laming coll.)

82.   We start our journey having crossed the bridge from the down platform to be greeted by this sign on the up one. We turn left and use the footpath featured in the next two photographs. (P.J.Kelley)

83.   A view north from Station Road shows the river passing under the centre arch and the engine shed on the right. Turn left at the end of the pavement to enter the station approach. The covered walkway leads to the Low Level platform. (P.Laming coll.)

84.   The panorama from an up signal post includes a gas holder, the engine shed and down platform extension in progress. Lower centre is the connection to Low Level and to the left of it is the footpath from the walkway. (D.Brennand coll.)

85.   The Low Level platform was just that in two senses. The connecting line descended at 1 in 50 behind it and reached the branch at the ground frame box in the distance. This housed nine levers; the photograph is from 29th July 1950. (K.Nunn/LCGB)

86.   The branch had some unusual stock with verandahs. See *Branch Line to Upwell* for earlier views and the film *The Titfield Thunderbolt* for later ones, but all the buffers would be present. The date is 5th May 1951, closure day. (A.J.Pike/F.Hornby coll.)

87.   The interior was recorded on the same day, with long leather straps for window adjustment in evidence. The layout facilitated the issue of tickets and the other coaches had end doors, plus drop plates. (J.J.Smith/R.M.Casserley coll.)

FEERING HALT

88.   This stop opened later than the others, on 1st January 1934. This northward view is from the 1930s and includes the multitude of telephone wires which served the Essex coastal area. The railway had only two wires. (Lens of Sutton coll.)

89.   A closer and later view reveals that passenger accommodation comprised a retired horse bus body. It was ex-LGOC Type B and included a parcels office, in its early days here. (D.T.Rowe)

90.   This was the vista encountered by your scribe in 1947, before requesting "half single to Tiptree please". My parents car awaited me and an unforgettable experience was had. One lamp sufficed, the contents being provided by the guard. (K.Nunn/LCGB)

91.   It is 12th August 1950 and the train crew will soon deal with the level crossing gates. The lower steps had to be removed before coaches left the branch. The leading one has six wheels and was one of the last six-wheelers still in use in Britain. (J.H.Meredith)

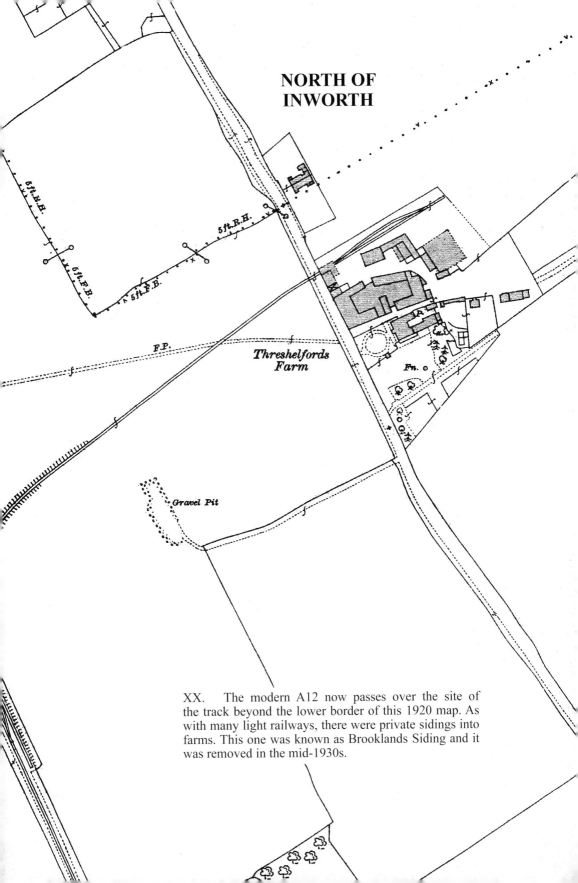

5ft.R.H.

5ft.R.H.

5ft.F.B.

5ft.F.B.

5ft.F.B.

F.P.

Threshelfords Farm

Fn. o

Gravel Pit

XX. The modern A12 now passes over the site of the track beyond the lower border of this 1920 map. As with many light railways, there were private sidings into farms. This one was known as Brooklands Siding and it was removed in the mid-1930s.

INWORTH

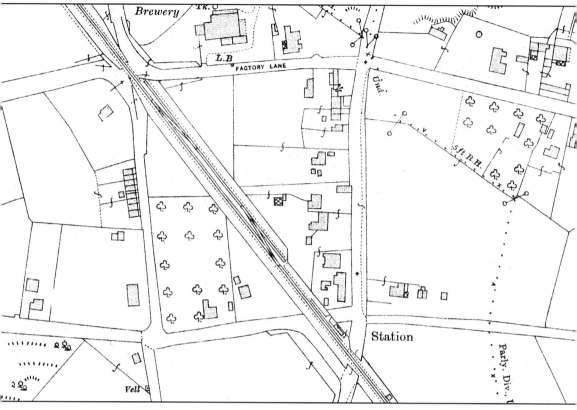

XXI. The 1922 edition features the goods loop known as Heath Siding. The village housed 667 in 1901 and 712 in 1951.

92. The old coach body arrived a few years after the station opened, following many complaints. However, there was the luxury of two oil lamps and two seats. (D.T.Rowe)

93.   The fireman thoughtfully made up his fire for the benefit of the photographer
on the final day of operation, 5th May 1951. Sadly the weather was awful.
(D.T.Rowe)

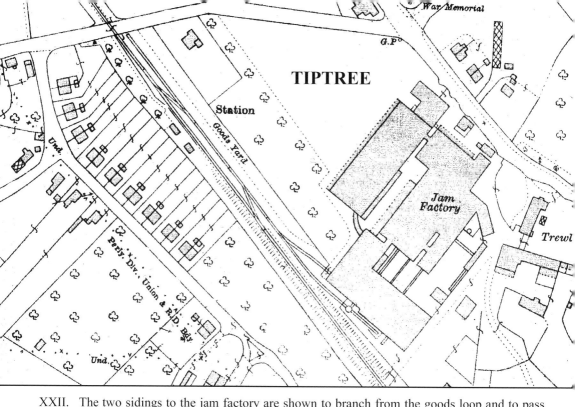

XXII. The two sidings to the jam factory are shown to branch from the goods loop and to pass through gates. "Semis" abound on this 1922 extract.

94. The famous Wilkin Jam Factory is in the background of this early photograph from the level crossing. The firm had first been known as Britannia Fruit Farms. (Wilkin Jam)

95.   The nameboard states "Tiptree Heath", but this term was never used. There is no seat and the carpenters are still at work and so one assumes that it was a mistake, which was rectified before opening. (R.M.Casserley coll.)

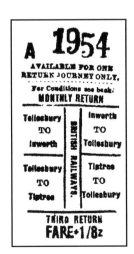

96.   The old jam factory sidings enter the top left buildings. The station and level crossing are top right. The population was 2453 when the line closed; it was under 800 when it opened. (Wilkin Jam)

B 0357

AVAILABLE FOR ONE
SINGLE JOURNEY ONLY.

For Conditions see back

Kelvedon TO Tiptree	L	Tiptree TO Kelvedon
	N	
Feering Halt TO Tiptree	E	Tiptree TO Feering Halt
	R	

THIRD SINGLE
FARE-9d.z

97.   Class J69 0-6-0T no. 68616 is coupled to a bogie saloon, a 6-wheeled 3rd class coach, another 6-wheeler (probably a jam van) and a brake van, on 12th August 1950. (J.H.Meredith)

98.   The waiting room was in the building on the right, oil lamps were kept in the centre one, while the one on the left was the parcels shed. (D.T.Rowe)

99. Class J69/1 0-6-0T no. 68616 has two saloons in tow on 7th August 1950, while we have the opportunity to see the length of the goods loop. Goods traffic continued here until 1st October 1962. (W.Dendy/ B.W.L.Brooksbank coll.)

100. Class J69 0-6-0T no. 68578 worked the 10.10am from Kelvedon on the last day of passenger operation. The boarded crossing was used for parcels and mailbags. Seldom had such a long train been operated. (D.T.Rowe)

TOLLESHUNT KNIGHTS

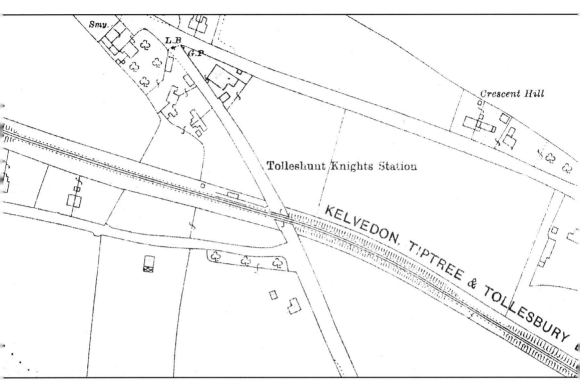

XXIII. After leaving Tiptree, trains descended at 1 in 50 towards the coastal plain and reached Tudwick Road Siding just before milepost 4. The siding was a public one on the north side and the line beyond here closed completely on 29th October 1951. There were then just over 400 residents in the village.

101.   This station opened on 12th December 1910 and had gates behind the camera which were operated by the train crew. After leaving the station, trains reached Church Siding, near milepost 5½. It was a loop on the north side of the line and it despatched peas and soft fruit in particular. (W.Dendy/B.W.L.Brooksbank coll.)

TOLLESHUNT D'ARCY

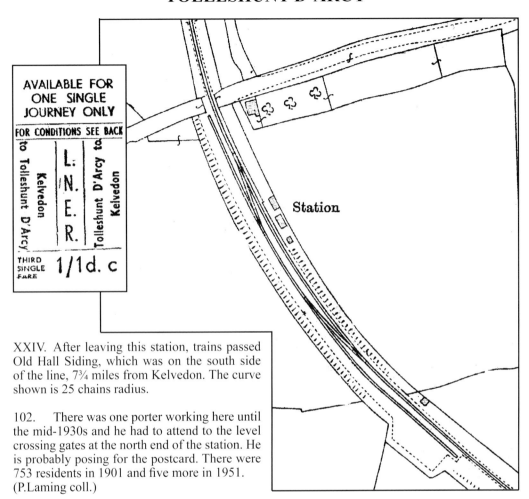

AVAILABLE FOR
ONE SINGLE
JOURNEY ONLY

FOR CONDITIONS SEE BACK

Kelvedon to Tolleshunt D'Arcy

L.
N.
E.
R.

Tolleshunt D'Arcy to Kelvedon

THIRD
SINGLE
FARE

1/1d. c

Station

XXIV. After leaving this station, trains passed Old Hall Siding, which was on the south side of the line, 7¾ miles from Kelvedon. The curve shown is 25 chains radius.

102.   There was one porter working here until the mid-1930s and he had to attend to the level crossing gates at the north end of the station. He is probably posing for the postcard. There were 753 residents in 1901 and five more in 1951. (P.Laming coll.)

103.   This record is thought to be from the 1920s and includes a parcels crossing to the platform, which was the standard 15ins high above rail level. (Lens of Sutton coll.)

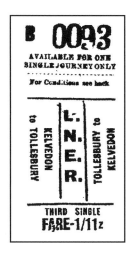

104.   It was unusual to have a grounded coach body as well as a building. It presumably made up for the lack of a parcels shed and was an ex-ECR four-wheeled third saloon. (P.Laming coll.)

105.   Another postcard view and this includes the level crossing and the roofless facility for gentlemen. Ladies were not considered on many light railways. (P.Laming coll.)

106.   The fireman watches his injector on 11th March 1950, as class J67/1 heads the lengthy 10.10am from Kelvedon. This locomotive had recently received BR's "Lion & Monocycle" emblem. (D.T.Rowe)

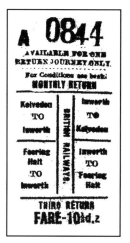

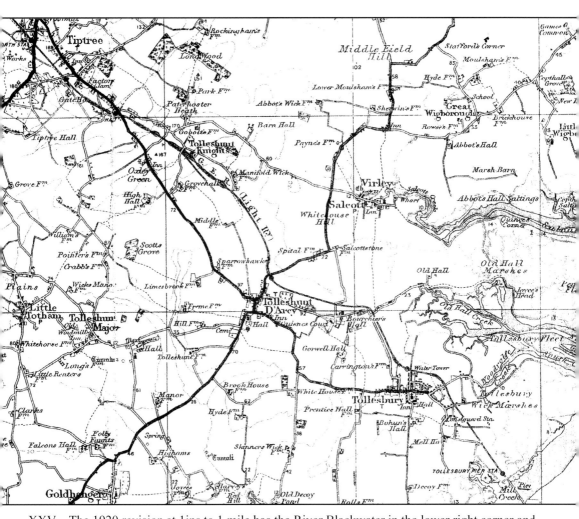

XXV.   The 1920 revision at 1ins to 1 mile has the River Blackwater in the lower right corner and the terminus very remote from habitation.

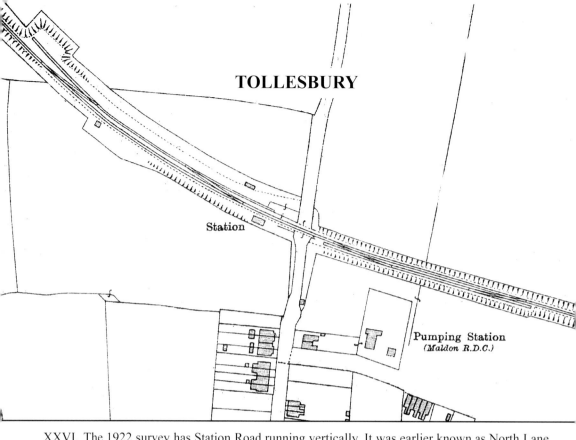

TOLLESBURY

Station

Pumping Station
(Maldon R.D.C.)

XXVI. The 1922 survey has Station Road running vertically. It was earlier known as North Lane and had an ungated level crossing. To the left of it is the goods yard and to the right is a run-round loop for use by trains terminating here.

107.   The first six views are from early postcards. We look across the goods siding to the now familiar standard buildings. It seems that the small one was provided as a porters room, but was mostly used as an oil and general store. (P.Laming coll.)

108. This animated scene was entitled "Waiting for the train at Tollesbury", but was it the first train? There were 1720 souls listed in 1901 and 1594 in 1951. (P.Laming coll.)

109. The card was annotated October 1904, the month of opening. The covering of sleepers with ballast was not allowed by that time and so there was work still to be done. The only cattle pen on the branch is evident. (Lens of Sutton coll.)

110.   This is probably a test train, as wagons were not often permitted between a locomotive and its coaches. They could follow in a "Mixed Train"; there was one such departure at 6.20pm in the first timetable. (P.Laming coll.)

111.   South of the station, there was a gated level crossing at Tollesbury Wick. This card included the words "Station & Waterworks, Tollesbury". More of the cattle dock is visible. (Lens of Sutton coll.)

112.   A picture from the 1920s features two ex-Upwell Tramway coaches, the far one having a guards ducket projecting slightly. (Lens of Sutton coll.)

113.   Class J68 0-6-0T no. 7048 is seen with the same coaches. Railings have replaced the wooden rails, but little else has changed. (Lens of Sutton coll.)

114.   The same (or similar) pair of coaches were recorded behind 0-6-0T no. 8636 on 8th January 1949. The line had six bogie coaches from the Wisbech & Upwell Tramway in 1928-29. They replaced the original eight ex-GER four-wheelers. Two six-wheelers came from the Stoke Ferry branch in 1931 and they ran to the end. (J.H.Meredith)

115.   There was a big demand for verandah space on the last train, the 7.22pm departure on 5th May 1951. The locomotive is class J69/1 0-6-0 no. 68578. (P.J.Kelley)

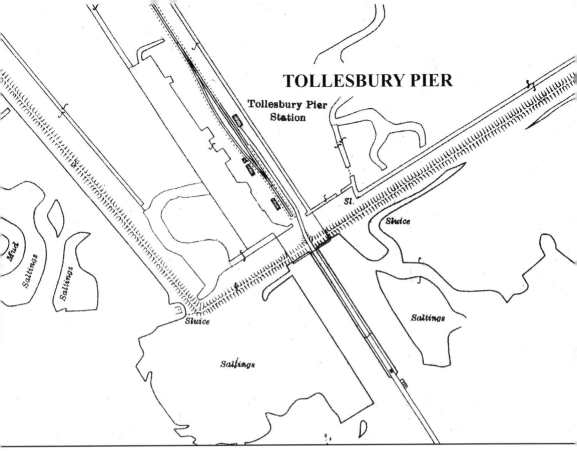

TOLLESBURY PIER

Tollesbury Pier
Station

Mud

Saltings

Saltings

Sl.

Sluice

Sluice

Saltings

Saltings

XXVII. The extension to the pier was late opening (May 1907) and early closing (July 1921). It is shown on the 1923 edition. In 1920, there were arrivals at 12.10 and 2.32, with departures at 12.20 and 2.43pm, "if required".

116. The featureless landscape is emphasised in this rare view of a passenger train near the terminus. No sidings were provided and the pier was only suitable for pedestrians.
(P.Laming coll.)

117.   There were high hopes of a major holiday venue being developed in this area in the Edwardian era, but "what you see is what you got" applied. No goods traffic was allowed. (P.Laming coll.)

118.   The standard building was again provided, with the firebuckets conveniently close to the convenience in a conventional configuration. The staff of one would be a lonely one. (P.Laming coll.)

119.   The pier was 1770ft long and, despite its length, the water was only 10ft deep at low tide at its extremity. It was breached early in World War II as an anti-invasion measure and the storm of February 1953 was its demise. It is seen in January 1949. (J.H.Meredith)

120.   The skeleton of a failed railway was not likely to create a best selling postcard, but it forms a fitting finale to a section dealing with the remains of a much loved railway branch, of great character. (R.M.Casserley coll.)

Easebourne Lane, Midhurst, West Sussex.
GU29 9AZ   Tel:01730 813169

www.middletonpress.co.uk   email:info@middletonpress.co.uk
A-978 0 906520 B-978 1 873793 C-978 1 901706 D-978 1 904474 E-978 1 906008

All titles listed below were in print at time of publication - please check current availability by looking at our website - *www.middletonpress.co.uk* or by requesting a Brochure which includes our *LATEST* RAILWAY TITLES also our TRAMWAY, TROLLEYBUS, MILITARY and WATERWAYS series